HELP YOUR CHILD FEEL HAPPIER

HELP YOUR CHILD FEEL HAPPIER

An Hachette UK Company
www.hachette.co.uk

Vie Books, an imprint of Summersdale Publishers Ltd
Part of Octopus Publishing Group Limited
Carmelite House
50 Victoria Embankment
LONDON
EC4Y 0DZ
UK

www.summersdale.com

Printed and bound in China

ISBN: 978-1-78783-664-8

Substantial discounts on bulk quantities of Summersdale books are available to corporations, professional associations and other organizations. For details contact general enquiries: telephone: +44 (0) 1243 771107 or email: enquiries@summersdale.com.

HELP YOUR CHILD FEEL HAPPIER

101 Ways to Boost Positivity and Self-Confidence

CAROLINE ROOPE

DISCLAIMER

Neither the author nor the publisher can be held responsible for any loss or claim arising out of the use, or misuse, of the suggestions made herein. None of the views or suggestions in this book is intended to replace medical opinion from a doctor. If you have concerns about your health or that of a child in your care, please seek professional advice.

CONTENTS

How to Use
This Book

If your child is struggling with feelings of unhappiness, don't panic. Take some time to sit with them and look through the tips in this book. Using a combination of practical advice and simple ideas that can be incorporated into everyday family life, you and your child can work together to manage their emotions and nurture a more positive outlook.

INTRODUCTION

Ask any parent the world over what they hope and dream for their child as they are growing up and the answer is universal: "I want them to feel loved and be happy." It sounds simple, but the reality can be more challenging. Too often we think of happiness as just a moment in time or a fleeting experience, but lasting contentment is much more complex. In a world where 10–20 per cent of children and adolescents are experiencing mental health disorders – with half of all mental health illnesses beginning by the age of 14* – making sure our children have a positive outlook on life has never been more important. Often it's hard to balance what's best for your child with allowing them the freedom to follow their own path, but if we can equip them with the skills to overcome setbacks, we can help to ensure that the path they choose to follow is paved with happiness and self-fulfilment.

*Source: World Health Organization

CHAPTER 1

Talking and Listening

Being able to communicate effectively is the keystone of a happy parent – child relationship – it nurtures our bond and encourages our children to listen to us. Talking openly about our feelings as a family allows us to support each other through the good times, as well as the tough ones.

What being unhappy looks like

Often a child's behaviour is a useful indicator of how they are feeling, particularly in the case of younger children, who may not have the vocabulary to put their feelings and emotions into words. Signs to look out for include:

- **Becoming withdrawn – or a usually quiet child becoming aggressive.**
- **Excessive mood swings.**
- **Complaining about physical problems, such as stomach- or headaches (rule out illness first).**
- **Changes in appetite.**
- **Sleep disturbances.**
- **Unwillingness to engage in their normal routine, such as not wanting to go to school or after-school clubs.**

Trust your instincts; you know your child best. If you feel that something isn't right, it's time to try to work out why.

Finding out why

It's crucial to find out the cause of your child's unhappiness so that together you can work towards a solution. Allow them to express how they are feeling, knowing that you are on their side. Try tracking your child's mood in a diary to see if there are any patterns – for instance, are they always upset after swimming club? Or just before school? Try to identify any triggers, but be mindful of belittling their emotions – a younger child's perspective is very different to our own and they may feel genuinely unhappy about something we consider trivial.

LET'S TALK ABOUT IT

Getting children to open up about what's bothering them can be hard. The questions we ask and the way we articulate them can often determine whether they feel comfortable sharing what's making them unhappy. Try not to pre-judge or assume that you know what is wrong. Rather than asking a direct question like: "Are you unhappy?", try saying, "I'm worried about you, as you don't seem yourself. Is there anything you'd like me to help you with?" The key to effective communication is to invite dialogue, rather than a straight "yes" or "no" answer.

Reset your tone

When we communicate with our children, the tone of what we are saying is just as important as the meaning of the words. They are very attuned to the pitch of our voices and are much more likely to respond positively when we use a soft and empathetic tone, as opposed to a harsh or critical one. When your words and tone come from a place of love and openness, that is what your child will hear, encouraging them to open up in return. You'll also be modelling effective communication – a skill your child will need throughout their life.

Mindful listening

How often do we stop and really listen to what our children are telling us? Shutting out the noise of everyday life, as well as our own inner voices, can be a challenge. In order to hear what they are really saying, we need to practise mindful listening. Try:

- **Clearing your mind before you talk to your child and really focusing on what they are saying.**
- **Ensuring that your thoughts aren't a block to hearing the message.**
- **Repeating back what your child said, so they know you were really listening. This also helps to foster connectedness.**

Mindful listening shows your child that what they have to say is valued. It enables them to feel confident about sharing any difficulties with you, which helps to strengthen the child–parent bond.

Tackling difficult conversations

Sometimes we need to have difficult conversations with our children, particularly if the source of their unhappiness is linked to harmful behaviours, such as alcohol or bullying. Tackling these difficult subjects together is a sign that you have a strong and trusting relationship. Try:

- Gathering your thoughts and staying calm.
- Not being judgemental or overly emotional.
- Listening mindfully.
- Asking open-ended questions.
- Thanking your child for coming to you.

If harmful behaviours are having a profound impact on your child's happiness, seek professional help at the earliest opportunity. The World Health Organization website has many useful resources related to mental health that are available to download at www.who.int.

CONFLICT MANAGEMENT

A barrier to feeling happy and having a positive outlook can sometimes come from conflict. An important part of growing up is learning how to resolve such situations; it's a necessary life skill. Often this process starts at home, where conflict arises naturally between family members – particularly siblings! Teaching our children how to tackle disputes with the people closest to them will help them to feel confident when resolving conflict in other areas of their life. Try the following steps next time you and your child have a disagreement to resolve:

- **Let your child have their say without interrupting.**

- **Explain your own feelings and views briefly and without blame, so that your child begins to learn the importance of other viewpoints.**

- **Encourage them to think of a solution or compromise.**

It's important to remember that some conflict with your child is normal and healthy, particularly as they start to form their own opinions.

Let your body do the talking

Positive non-verbal communication helps to nurture long-lasting emotional bonds with our children. Warm and caring body language tells them that we want to be close and it also helps to strengthen verbal messages. As well as hugs, kisses and touching your child affectionately, you can also help young kids understand body language with some games; for example:

• Watch their favourite TV programme with the sound off and help them to interpret the emotions that the characters might be feeling.

• Use toys to act out emotions and role-play different scenarios to help them recognize other people's feelings.

Assisting your child to see that communication involves our whole body, rather than just the words we speak, will enable them to form stronger connections with those around them.

When your child says "I can't"

All children will utter these words at some point
– after all, we all have moments of despondency,
even grown-ups! Helping your child to change
their mindset to "I can..." starts with your initial
response. Empathize by saying, "I know you are
finding this hard" – it shows your child that you
recognize their struggle. For example, if they are
finding it hard to master a motor skill, such as
using a knife and fork, try linking their difficulty
to a family story to help them feel that they're
not alone: "Have I ever told you how clumsy I
am when I'm eating?" Finally, remind them that
they can't do it yet, but you will help them to
find a solution.

When you say "don't"

The word "don't" is probably one of the most frequently used when we're parenting our children. We often know what we *don't* want to happen in a situation and before we know it, the word, with all of its negative meanings, has slipped out of our mouths. The problem is that it doesn't promote positive behaviour. Try switching "don'ts" to "dos"; for example:

- "Don't snatch that toy" becomes "Please pass the toy nicely."

- "Don't leave your towel on the bathroom floor" becomes "Please hang up your towel."

- "Don't be unkind to your brother" becomes "Show kindness to your brother."

By placing the emphasis on the positive aspect of the request, we can empower our children to respond with a positive action and nurture their sense of self-belief.

POSITIVE FEEDBACK WORD BANK

Children thrive on positive feedback and words of encouragement. Try to use some of these phrases and words to foster a sense of love and appreciation.

- **"That's wonderful."**
- **"I like the way you did that."**
- **"I'm pleased with/proud of you."**
- **"You showed great resilience when you ____."**
- **"Way to go."**

And don't forget to show them, too! You could...

- **High-five them.**
- **Give them a pat on the arm or shoulder.**
- **Laugh with them.**
- **Hug them.**
- **Stroke their cheek or head.**

Encouraging our children through positive words and actions not only increases their confidence levels, but also helps to nurture positive self-talk, thus reinforcing their sense of inner happiness.

Meeting in the middle

We've all been there: the battle of wills at bedtime, wearing suitable clothing when it's near Arctic conditions outside, choosing fruit instead of sweets – parenting really is the art of compromise! Crucially, this also teaches our children a valuable life skill; and if we can all learn to compromise, we'll find that family life becomes happier. Encourage your child to see other people's points of view and approach the situation with a win–win attitude. Help them to find a solution so that everyone achieves a successful outcome. The mantra "pick your battles" really comes into its own here!

Tune in to their talking rituals

Does your child have a time of day when they talk non-stop? Are they quiet in the morning but full of chatter in the evening? Perhaps they enjoy a lively exchange – or do they prefer discussions at a slower pace? Respect their natural rhythms for talking and use those moments to nurture openness and connection, without any pressure. By understanding their talking rituals, you'll be able to choose the right moment to engage with them and strengthen the bond we achieve through effective communication.

What's the story?

Emotional literacy is just as important as academic literacy and when the two combine, our children manage to relate an experience or situation from beginning to end. This is crucial to explain something they are finding difficult, and effectively convey what feelings and emotions they are experiencing. In turn, this enables us to help them solve the problem.

Ask questions such as: "What happened next?", "What did you say?" and "How did you feel?" so that your child knows you are interested in what they are saying. Giving undivided attention in this way shows them that they are valued and important to us.

CHAPTER 2

Cultivating a Positive Mindset

An important part of growing up is acknowledging that life doesn't always go to plan. For some children disappointment can lead to self-doubt and sadness. By encouraging a positive mindset, we can help them to reshape how they feel about themselves, thus giving them the resilience to weather life's storms.

25

KEEP A GRATITUDE JOURNAL

Reminding our children of the things we are thankful for can be a great way to foster positivity. By keeping a gratitude journal when times are tough, kids will feel encouraged to reflect on the joy that life brings. All you need is a notebook. Give your child prompts, such as: "What made you laugh today?" or "What was the best part of your day?" – it's a great opportunity to improve writing skills, too! Younger children could draw something that made them happy instead. Don't be disheartened if they write "eating ice-cream" or "watching TV". Children's perceptions of gratitude often differ wildly from ours!

Acknowledge achievement the right way

Praise needs to have a purpose. It's easy just to say "great job" or "well done" when your child achieves something, but by focusing on the effort they put in rather than the outcome, we can reinforce the idea that success comes from hard work. This is crucial in building optimism and a positive mindset. Try to avoid phrases like, "You got all of your spelling test right? Wow, you're so clever!" Instead, focus on the effort: "I'm so proud of the work you put into learning your spellings." By cultivating our children's sense of self-belief we'll also be nurturing their inner happiness.

Mindset mantras

Mantras can help to develop self-awareness, as well as a positive mindset. They work like a personal good-news boost; and it's true that whatever we hear the most of, we start to believe. Help your child to develop their own set of mantras that they can repeat to themselves to boost their self-esteem. They should be short and positive, such as: "I am loving" and "I am unique." You could also write some positive statements about your child, such as: "I believe in you", and slip them into their lunchbox or school bag for an extra boost.

Help your child to identify their strengths

Create a strength chain so that your child has a visible reminder of the things they are good at. Cut out strips of paper and ask your child to write one of their strengths on each one. Don't forget that character traits such as being a good friend are just as important as being good at sport. Link each piece of paper together using sticky tape and hang the chain up. You can add new links each time your child develops a new strength. By encouraging them to identify their own unique abilities, you'll be helping them to build self-esteem and self-awareness.

HELPING OTHERS

People who volunteer or help others in need have been found to have greater feelings of well-being and a more positive outlook than those who don't. Therefore, by encouraging your child to be helpful, you will be giving them a chance to feel good about themselves. Helping others also fosters connectedness and encourages us to build positive relationships with those around us. For older children, supporting an elderly neighbour or helping a friend with schoolwork can be a way to promote feelings of positivity. Even very young children can be encouraged to get stuck in by picking up toys. Don't forget to praise their efforts and hard work!

Make a plan

Planning is a great way to ensure we stay on track when we're trying to achieve something. This is especially true when attempting to accomplish something new or challenging. Encourage your child to set themselves goals and write a plan of how they can achieve them. Make sure they consider what obstacles they might come up against and what the impact could be. Having a plan makes it more likely that your child will succeed, which in turn will boost their confidence and foster a positive attitude.

Take small steps

Break a challenge down into smaller steps and it becomes less daunting. Draw a ladder and ask your child to write what they are finding challenging at the top. Next, encourage them to think about what smaller steps they can take to reach their goal and write them on each step. For instance, if they are worried about speaking in class, practising on their own could be the first step. The next step could be to practise in front of a parent, and so on, until they reach the top. Building up their confidence with each step will equip them with the positive mindset needed to tackle the challenge.

Share your experiences

Make sharing your positive experiences as a family part of your daily routine. You could do this at dinnertime or any other moment when you are all together. It's also a good opportunity to talk about what didn't go to plan. A problem shared is a problem halved and talking openly with each other about the challenges of the day is a good way to troubleshoot anything your child is finding difficult. Encourage them to think of some solutions, giving examples from your own experiences, to help them achieve a positive outcome.

EMBRACE ANTICIPATION

It's official: that "Friday feeling" really does exist! Research has found that most of us prefer Fridays to any other day of the week, most likely because we look forward to a fun and restful weekend. Embrace the excitement of anticipation – start a family calendar and record all the positive events you have to look forward to. Visiting grandparents, family outings and holidays are much more likely to promote a positive mindset than a dentist appointment! Talk regularly with your child about what's coming up, so they have something to look forward to.

Help them to feel comfortable with their emotions

Allow your child the freedom to express how they feel. Teach them how to laugh, feel joyful and be thankful, but also to cry and feel frustrated. Crying is a healthy way for both children and adults to express negative emotions; doing so is as much a part of the human experience as laughing and feeling happy. The most important thing we can do as parents is create an environment where they feel safe communicating their feelings, both positive and negative. While it's hard to see our children upset, fostering a culture where they can be open about their emotions helps to strengthen relationships at their very core.

Say "yes"

Or, at least, if a "yes" is completely out of the question ("Can I jump out of the window?" springs to mind!), try to reframe your response to initiate a positive conversation. For instance, you might ask them, "If you were a parent, what would convince you to allow your child to jump out of the window?" Doing this will engage your child in a meaningful conversation that highlights the decision-making process. The answer will sometimes still be "no", but instead of a negative response, offer up a question that will make them stop and think.

Positivity poster

Create a positivity poster! A strong visual message can help to remind the whole family to think positively. Get together and choose a quote from a book or use the internet to research a saying that can become a family mantra, such as Roald Dahl's famous quote: "If you have good thoughts, they will shine out of your face like sunbeams." Write it in the centre of the poster and decorate the space around it with images of things that make you all feel happy. Younger children can draw their happy pictures or colour in the poster. Hang it somewhere where everyone can see it and start thinking positively!

HUGS AND HIGH-FIVES

Cultivate an environment of happiness and positivity by watching funny movies and reading funny books. Tell jokes and share family stories that have happy endings. Smile at each other, laugh together and use kind words. Make sure every day is filled with hugs, kisses and high-fives. It goes without saying that a loved child is a happy child – and giving them extra cuddles and love is definitely not a hardship! After all, what could be better than a big, squishy hug with the people you love most in the world?

Seeking support

There may be occasions when a child's negative mindset becomes too overwhelming for you to manage without additional support. If your child's negativity has spiralled and is having a profound effect on their lives, and the lives of those around them, it's time to seek professional help. The key to positive thinking is acknowledging a tricky situation and looking at it productively – and that applies to adults, too. If your child needs professional help, speak to your family doctor to find out what support is available in your area.

CHAPTER 3

Creating a Positive Self-Image

Encouraging your child to value themselves is one of the greatest gifts a parent can give. Children with a sense of self-worth grow into happy, balanced adults. More importantly, it helps them to overcome mistakes, supporting them to do well at school, at home and in relationships.

41

Challenge negative thoughts

Children are often their own harshest critics, and over time thoughts such as: "I'm stupid" or "I'm a bad friend" can lead to low self-esteem and a negative self-image. Try encouraging your child to challenge their inner critic – ask them to write down their negative thought and then interrogate it. For instance, "Is this based on fact? Where is the evidence?" and "Is this just my opinion?" This will help them to determine whether their thoughts are rational and, crucially, learn not to accept every thought as fact.

Positive thinking

When your child makes a mistake or finds something tricky, it can have an impact on their entire day. Try to encourage them to think about what they can learn from it and then move on. Dwelling on negative situations can easily lead to anxiety. Instead, focus on the positive experiences they've had; for example:

- At the end of every day, ask your child to write down three things that went well. These could be as simple as a good drawing, playing with a friend or finishing a challenging project.

- Then ask your child to write what they did to make them happen. This encourages them to see the value in their effort, helping to build confidence and self-esteem.

By teaching our children the resilience to reflect, move on and see positive outcomes, we'll be nurturing a happier outlook – a skill that will help them throughout life.

BEING BODY POSITIVE

Fact: people come in all shapes and sizes. Diversity is what makes being human so amazing, and it's our role as parents to help our children to develop a healthy attitude towards their own bodies and other people's. This starts with us and how we perceive ourselves. Negative talk about our own appearance, no matter how flabby we think we are, can be detrimental if we're within earshot of our children. Be kind to yourself – teach them that there is no wrong body, just different bodies, and that beauty comes from within.

Healthy habits

By teaching children to respect their bodies, we're helping to instil the importance of a healthy mind and body. Nurture good habits by:

- Guiding them towards activities that make them happy. If they're not keen on structured pursuits or classes, just going for a bike ride or kicking a ball still counts! Praise them for their efforts and achievements.

- Building positive connections with food – make healthy eating fun by cooking together. Talk to them about where the food came from and what makes something healthy (or not!).

- Not banning things like ice-cream entirely; instead, use it to show healthy portioning.

Encouraging our children to embrace healthy habits when they are young can have a positive impact on the choices they make as they grow up.

It's what's inside that counts

Anxiety in children is in many instances linked to feelings of inadequacy and low self-esteem. Even without parental pressure, children often feel they have to look a certain way or be the best in class to be successful. Help your child to see that their value goes beyond all of this – praising them for who they are helps to build self-esteem, which in turn leads to a happier outlook. Try asking them to write down five character traits that they like about themselves, such as friendliness, being helpful, etc., and use that to start a conversation about valuing similar attributes in others.

Social media

Social media is often accused of giving a distorted view of what "normal" looks like. It's really important that we explain to children, particularly as they approach their teenage years, that online images only show a snapshot of someone's life – and that selfies and other headshots may have been airbrushed or "filtered" to look a certain way. Spend some time browsing with your child for "before" and "after" images online, and talk about the differences. It's also important to balance this with the positive effect that appropriate use of social media can have on our children's lives, as a way to connect with friends and make sense of the world around them.

CHOICES, CHOICES

Help your child to feel empowered and give their self-confidence a boost by giving them the right to choose — within a reasonable set of options, of course! For young children, this could be as simple as giving them some alternatives for lunch, and letting them choose what they like, or letting them pick their clothes for the day, even if that ends up being a superhero cape and pants! For older children it could be choosing how to spend their pocket money. This gets them thinking about consequences and taking responsibility for their own decisions. By allowing your child the autonomy to choose, you'll be reinforcing the message that you have confidence in them, which in turn helps them to build a positive self-image.

Helping around the house

By asking your child to help around the house, you'll not only be teaching them practical life skills, but you'll also be giving them the opportunity to demonstrate their competence. In turn, they will feel that their contribution to family life is valuable, helping to raise their self-esteem. Start when they are young by letting them watch you and then making it a game — "I bet you can't make your bed before I come back." With reluctant older children you might need to offer a small incentive or reward, but start young enough and it'll soon become the norm!

Let them off the leash

To build confidence, children have to take chances. So take a deep breath and stand back! It's easy in theory, but in practice letting your child off the leash can feel a little daunting. Next time you feel compelled to jump in and rescue them from a situation, pause for a moment and consider whether they really need your input (unless they are doing something dangerous). Could they learn a valuable life lesson from being left to their own devices? Even if the outcome isn't what was intended, they may just learn a few problem-solving skills along the way.

Praise your child

When praise is specific and appropriately given, it becomes a valuable tool for nurturing self-esteem. Keep a file or document wallet of their achievements – good school reports, their name appearing on a school-play programme, positive notes and feedback from teachers or anything they are particularly proud of, no matter how small. If they have a bad day, take out the file and read it together, focusing on the effort they put in to secure their achievements.

TURN THE TABLES

It may seem counter-intuitive, but have you considered asking your child for their advice on a problem of your own? Discussing our own personal challenges in front of our children is a healthy way to show that it's OK to find things difficult. Asking them how they might approach the issue encourages all-important problem-solving skills and listening to their advice or opinion respectfully (no matter how bonkers it might sound!) will help them to feel valued.

TIP
40

Playtime

For younger children, spending time playing with their parents sends the message: "You are worth my time. I value you." Not only do young children learn through play, but it also helps to nurture feelings of self-worth, particularly if you allow them to choose the game or activity. Older children can benefit from "playtime" with us, too – whether that's a game of football in the park or a family splash-about in the local swimming pool. The key is to show that quality time with them is time well spent. We can also learn about our children through our interactions with them. Give your full focus to your child – you'll be surprised how quickly they can sense that you have "tuned out" – and you'll both benefit from special time together.

Foster a sense of belonging

Fostering a strong sense of belonging in our children helps them to know and recognize the support and love that surround them in their family unit. Encourage them to see this support network like a tree – the strong roots of their family (i.e. their parents or carers) allow the trunk (them) to grow strong. Knowing they are surrounded by people they can rely on helps children to feel happy and secure. Try writing a family statement or declaration and hang it where you can all see it; an example could be: "In our family we work hard to achieve our goals."

Encourage assertiveness

Being assertive means being able to speak up for ourselves in a way that is honest, but also respectful. It's a healthy way to communicate, as it sends the message that we're confident and believe in ourselves. Try the following with your child:

- Suggest they write down and mentally practise what they want to say.

- Ask them to stand up straight, put their shoulders back, look up and make eye contact.

- When they are ready to speak, encourage them to say what they want, clearly and politely.

- Remind them that they don't need to apologize if they are asking for something they need.

Encourage your child to see that learning to communicate in this way is a life skill they can use whenever they find it difficult to speak up for themselves.

CHAPTER 4

Mood Boosters

We all have good days and bad days. Children, in particular, can be prone to mood swings because they have not yet developed the emotional language to express how they are feeling. If your child needs an extra pick-me-up, try some of the following tips to help banish the blues.

UNLEASH YOUR INNER ROCK STAR

Music has long been known to have a positive effect on kids. If your child has a favourite piece of music that you know will bring a smile to their face, put it on and have a sing-along. There's something about belting out a tune that is brilliantly cathartic! Even better, help your child to make up some dance moves to go with it – bonus points if you manage not to fall over while practising...!

Go for a walk

Walking, particularly in nature, can have an instant positive effect on our mood. It has obvious physical benefits, too, and reminds us how lucky we are to have fresh air in our lungs and how precious our planet is. It's also good for engaging in a meaningful conversation with your child about the world around them. Make it fun by encouraging them to look out for different trees, sounds and textures. If you're lucky enough to be near a woodland, simple things like building dens and playing hide-and-seek in the trees can be enjoyed by all ages.

Get creative in the kitchen

Let your child pick their favourite dish and get cooking! Better still, help to improve their organizational skills by planning a menu or creating a recipe. Cooking together is a sociable experience with an enjoyable outcome (hopefully). If it doesn't turn out as expected (try not to pull a face!), encourage them to consider what they might do differently next time. This helps to foster problem-solving skills. If your child is older, why not let them do it independently? It'll be a great opportunity to build up their self-esteem and sense of achievement – as well as developing a valuable life skill.

Start a
family ritual

Do you always go to the sweet shop after school on a Friday? Or perhaps you always have pancakes for breakfast on a Sunday? Or maybe you have a special greeting or way of honouring your child's achievements? Creating family traditions helps to make a child feel secure and part of something special. The significance comes from the fact that the meaning is understood only by your children and you – like a secret language. This sense of shared experience helps to strengthen family bonds and you'll be making happy memories together, too.

FAMILY TIME

Finding the time for regular family activities is one of the best ways to boost happiness levels and share a positive experience together. If you can find something you all enjoy (adults included) then that's all the better. Movie nights in pyjamas can work well for all ages; or perhaps there's a sport you all enjoy, such as football or cycling. A regular board-games night could be fun – as long as there are no sore losers among you! Whatever your interests, spending time together as a family is essential in creating a lasting bond and boosting everyone's mood.

How does your garden grow?

Growing plants and flowers with your children is a fantastic way to teach responsibility. It has the benefit of providing a very visual example of how, with care and nurture, a small seed can grow into something strong and beautiful. It also helps to give a sense of achievement, as your child can see the results of their hard work. If you're short on space, you could try growing herbs or vegetables on a windowsill — cress is particularly easy to maintain and you can even give it a haircut for fun!

Find your inner child

Children are always delighted when a parent stops being their usual sensible self and acts a bit silly. Particularly if it's a surprise! Next time your child is having a pillow fight, or playing chase or "the floor is lava", why not join in, too? Getting inside their games is good for bonding and creating shared experiences. It's also important for our children to see us laughing and having time off from being a grown-up – and it's good for our mental health, too, if we can take a break from "adulting" and spend some time "childing" instead!

Start
something new

Hobbies help children to develop life skills that go beyond what they learn at school, and fortunately there are so many activities to choose from that there's usually something to suit everyone! Whether it's building model aeroplanes, crafting, reading books, coding or collecting, the benefits come from the skills that are formed through engaging in these hobbies. Also, they are great for stress busting and for fostering a sense of accomplishment. Often hobbies develop organically from your child's interests, but if not, let them choose something they enjoy – and let them lead the discussion. You might also see some future talents emerging; nurture these now and who knows where they'll lead them later in life.

TURN OFF THE GADGETS!

Technology is a huge and unavoidable part of our lives, but sometimes it can feel like it's getting in the way of the family time we need to boost positivity. If you're struggling to separate your child from a gadget, try the following:

- **Set an example by putting your own phone or tablet to one side. Establish set times for screens and stick to them — make your children part of the discussion, so they feel they've had an input.**

- **Make mealtimes a no-gadget zone.**

- **Remind them that there's a whole world out there — and they're missing it!**

If we can communicate our expectations and get the balance right (and that includes parents, too!), we'll have more time together to enjoy the things that make us feel happy.

Active body, healthy mind

Being active is an essential part of child development. Not only does it ensure our children stay physically healthy, but it's also an important mood booster. Try some of these ideas to make sure your child is making the most of their active time:

- Be a good active role model yourself.
- Involve the whole family and make it sociable.
- Introduce an element of competition – kids versus parents, garden games, etc.
- Exercise by stealth – park further away from school and walk some of the way.
- Give presents that promote activity, such as rollerblades, a tennis set, frisbees, a scooter, etc.

Learning to master physical skills also helps to build confidence, no matter what age we are, and makes us feel good about ourselves!

Time with friends

Spending time with friends is an essential part of growing up and a fabulous mood booster. Making sure your child has a support network outside of the family unit ensures they have access to a wider breadth of life experiences, as well as giving them the opportunity to socialize and learn from children of different backgrounds. Make sure your child has regular playdates or meet-ups and suggest outdoor play, where possible. If your child is older, encourage them to surround themselves with people they trust and who make them feel secure.

Laugh out loud

Get giggling! Numerous studies have shown that laughing out loud really is good for our mood. Sharing a funny moment also helps to connect with those around us, and being able to laugh at ourselves is an essential part of learning resilience and dealing with challenges in life. Initiate a tickling fight, play some silly games or just tell some silly jokes – anything that elicits a good belly-laugh will help to boost happiness levels. Watching a funny movie together or having a "who can create the craziest costume" competition allows all of us to just enjoy the moment – embrace it!

GET CREATIVE

Creative activities can provide an instant mood lift, if your child is feeling a little low. Creativity comes in so many different shapes and forms that there's generally something to suit everyone, whether it's painting, writing or crafting – the only limit is children's own imagination. Here are some ideas:

- **Ask them, "If you could be any animal, what would you be?"**
- **Make a card for someone close to them.**
- **Write a song and perform it to someone in your family (hairbrushes make great fake microphones).**
- **Design a planet and some new life forms to inhabit it.**

Encouraging kids to focus on the creative process will help them appreciate the whole experience, not just the end result.

Time out

Sometimes we all just need some breathing space — that means creating a quiet space where we feel secure, so we can relax without the distractions of everyday life. If your child is feeling overwhelmed and would benefit from some alone time, respect their decision and give them the space they crave. Having moments on our own, with or without silence, gives our brains time to process our thoughts and feelings. It also gives us time to reflect and recharge our internal batteries. If your child craves solitude, create a den or special place they can escape to when needed.

CHAPTER 5

Ways to Help Your Child Relax

When anxiety becomes overwhelming, knowing how to find a sense of inner calm is essential. If we teach our children relaxation skills when they are young, we can equip them with a tool they can use their entire life. Next time your child seems agitated, try these ideas.

Counting equals calmness

Counting can be a great way to readjust our minds and take a moment away from a stressful situation. Ask your child to choose a number – preferably over ten – and count to it slowly, taking a deep breath in with each digit and out between digits. Another way of using counting to be calm is to ground your child in their surroundings, using their senses – ask them to look for five things they can see, four things they can hear, three things they can feel, two things they can smell and one thing they can taste. When they've finished, ask them if they feel calmer and encourage them to try it next time they feel anxious.

Make (and use) a calming jar

Good for younger children, calming jars are easy to make and surprisingly effective! Watching the glitter fall to the bottom can have an instant calming effect, as your child takes a moment to refocus and clear their mind. All you need is a clean, empty jar, glitter paint or glue and some warm water. Put the glitter in first, then pour in the water. Seal the lid with superglue so there are no leaks. Finally, give it a shake and watch the glitter float. As it settles, encourage your child to settle their mind, too.

PROGRESSIVE MUSCLE RELAXATION

Progressive muscle relaxation encourages your child to squeeze their muscles in turn and then let them relax, feeling the tension drain away. Turn it into a game:

> **"Pretend you have a wet sponge in your hand. Squeeze all the water out. Squeeze really hard, then let it fall. See how much better your hands and arms feel when they're not clenched? Next, pretend you're standing in a muddy puddle. Push your feet down into the mud. Use every part of your legs to help you and spread out your toes. Then let it go. Feel the mud drain away. Great job!"**

Explain to your child that reducing the tension in our bodies helps us to reduce the tension in our minds, too.

Breathing

Breathing for relaxation is different to "ordinary" breathing. When we're using it to relax, we become conscious of each breath, which becomes a tool to release tension and improve our mood. Try the following:

- Ask your child to take a big, slow breath in.

- Tell them to breathe out slowly, thinking of how they feel at that moment.

- Another big, slow breath in.

- Ask them to breathe out again, this time thinking of things that make them happy.

- Another big, slow breath in.

- Finally, on the last breath out, ask them to think of how they want to feel.

Calm breathing also gives your child a sense of control and an anchor to hold on to if they're feeling anxious. Best of all, they can do it anywhere and at any time they need to.

Stretching

Like progressive muscle relaxation, stretching helps to reduce tension in our muscles. Ask your child to stretch their arms above their head and stand on tiptoe, like they are a puppet being pulled up by its string. Encourage them to make themselves as tall as possible and then flop back down. It's useful for younger children to be able to visualize the stretch, so ask them to imagine that they are a cat or reaching up to touch the stars. Repeat several times to get the full benefit.

Take a mindful moment

Mindfulness is about being present in the moment. It encourages us to engage in our surroundings, by actively using all of our senses so we can experience the "here and now". It provides us with a clearer and calmer mindset with which to go about our day. If your child is feeling anxious, ask them to focus on the things around them instead – what can they smell? What colours can they see? Can they hear anything? How does it make them feel? Encouraging your child to be mindful of their environment can help to refocus their thoughts, promoting positivity and well-being.

VISUALIZE SOMETHING HAPPY

Visualization is about creating a mental image of something we want to achieve or that makes us happy. The theory goes that when focusing on our goals by visualizing them clearly in the form of an image, we are more likely (and more determined) to make them happen. Try these steps:

1. **Find somewhere comfortable and quiet.**

2. **Ask your child to close their eyes and create an image in their mind — it could be as simple as a peaceful beach scene.**

3. **Encourage them to include all the senses, so the image is as real as possible. They don't need to share this information with you — it's just for them.**

Using our imagination in this way — especially combined with calm breathing — really is the easiest way to relax. You could try it at bedtime, too, if your child struggles with settling their mind before they go to sleep.

Healthy sleep habits

Developing good sleep habits is essential for our well-being during our waking hours. Children who get quality sleep are more likely to have a good attention span and a greater capacity to learn, and they are better behaved. Not only that: sleep performs a vital role in helping our minds to rest and recover.

- Stick to a routine – bath, brush, book, bed. If your child knows what to expect, they are less likely to be unsettled, making it easier for them to wind down.

- Make sure your child is active during the day and gets plenty of fresh air.

- Avoid overloading the latter part of the day with activities. Instead, have quiet time to help them settle.

- The glare from screens can inhibit sleep, so limit screen time in the evening – have family time instead!

It often takes a little while to establish a bedtime routine, particularly if it is new to your child. Have patience – when it comes to bedtime, it's definitely a case of "perseverance pays off"!

Yoga

Yoga encourages self-esteem and coordination, as well as flexibility and strength. Try these two animal-themed poses with your child:

- **Lion pose — kneel on a mat and sit back on your heels. Press your palms into your knees, splaying out your fingers like claws. Breathe in through your nose while opening your mouth, stretching your tongue down to your chin. Breathe out with a roar!**

- **Frog pose – go onto your hands and knees. Walk your knees out wide as far as possible, but don't overstretch. Bring your elbows and forearms to the ground beneath your shoulders, while keeping your palms flat.**

If your child enjoyed these yoga poses, you could see what classes are available in your area or download a yoga app and learn some more at home.

Do some colouring

There's a reason adult colouring books have become so popular over the past few years. Colouring is a mindful task that allows us the time and space to refocus our thoughts – and it works for adults just as much as it does for children. Next time your child is feeling anxious and needs time to relax, grab a colouring book – or print some colouring pages from the internet – find some crayons or felt tips and get colouring! Join in, too, and enjoy the shared benefits of bonding time and relaxation.

ENJOY A HOT BATH

Loved by adults and kids alike, bath time is a chance to help your child relax. There's nothing like the sensation of slipping into a bathtub full of hot water and bubbles, particularly after a busy or stressful day. Add their favourite bath foam to the water and, if they are young, a few simple toys – and allow them all the time they need (or until the water gets cold!). If your child is older and still comfortable having a parent with them at bath time, you could read to them or talk to them about their day.

Chasing clouds

Something as simple as watching the clouds drifting by can be incredibly relaxing. Not only does it encourage children to take their mind off other things, but it's also a great reminder of how amazing nature and planet Earth really are. Grab a blanket, find an open space where you can lie down and see if your child can spot any shapes or interesting features (you might be able to sneak some geography in there, too!). Try some breathing exercises (see page 77) as well for ultimate relaxation.

Get moving

Channel the nervous energy that comes with anxiety into getting active. Exercise is a fantastic mood booster and it also helps us to relax, thanks to all the feel-good endorphins that are released as we move our bodies. Even simple, repetitive movements, such as ten jumping jacks or hopping on the spot for a few moments, can be enough to give us a mental boost. It's also a good distraction from whatever is worrying your child and helps them to think about something else.

Stay calm

As adults, modelling the ability to be calm shows our children the importance of a healthy mind. Kids also look to us to learn how to react in different situations, picking up on our signals and cues — so if we are anxious, our child will pick up on that anxiety and feel even more nervous. Making the decision to manage our child's anxiety requires managing our own anxiety, too. This means that we need to employ some of the techniques discussed in this chapter, as well as moderating our tone and facial expressions when we are stressed and our children are present.

CHAPTER 6

Skills for Life

Setting our children up for their future goes beyond practical skills – although those are of course important. Ensuring that our children are emotionally and mentally prepared to navigate their way through the challenges that life throws at them will help to safeguard their future happiness, too.

FRIENDSHIPS

Learning how to make friends is a key part of child development. Friendships provide children with an opportunity to learn how to interact and communicate with the people around them, as well as skills such as problem-solving, resolution and forgiveness. Help your child to form healthy friendships by:

- **Encouraging the relationships that are important to them and supporting them in their choice.**

- **Respecting their personality – they might like a big circle of friends or prefer the company of a few special pals; neither is right or wrong.**

- **Modelling healthy friendships yourself.**

Having friends is good for a child's self-esteem and confidence, which means it's good for their happiness levels, too!

Building meaningful relationships

Teaching your child to build warm and responsive relationships, both with their family and with their friends, is essential for well-being and happiness. Relationships affect all areas of child development, as well as influencing how children view the world and themselves, so it's really important we invest time in making them positive experiences. We can do this by:

- Showing them that we're interested in their activities.

- Encouraging them to express their emotions and respecting their feelings when they do.

- Making space for uninterrupted, unstructured time with them every day.

- Providing opportunities for them to make friends.

Nurturing the bond we have with our child is the best way to show them how to build strong relationships with others.

Learning to think critically

Life is complex in many ways, and learning to make decisions and analyze information are crucial life skills. The ability to ask and find the "why" in things is an essential element of critical thinking. The best way for young children to develop this skill is through play. Make sure they have plenty of opportunities to try out ideas, formulate a plan, take a risk, make mistakes and work out a solution. Older children should be encouraged to question what they see, particularly online and on social media, and form decisions through evaluation and research.

Resilience

Resilience is a necessary life skill — knowing how to face up to life's challenges, bounce back from a failure and try again can be learned with a little input from us. Children feel safe to take on a difficult task when we provide the right environment for them — one of love, support and structure. Encourage your child to try new things and offer a new challenge when the previous one is mastered. Praise them for their effort, rather than the outcome, e.g. "I love it that you kept trying the monkey bars, even when you fell off. Great job."

When children are resilient, they are more likely to be curious about the world and feel braver in the face of adversity. We cannot change the challenges our children might face in the future, but if we can equip them with the right tools, we can give them the best possible chance to overcome them.

COMMUNICATION

Providing opportunities for your child to communicate and interact will show them the importance of listening to and understanding others. Children need interactions with other people every day to nurture healthy social-emotional skills. For younger children, reading social cues, such as acknowledging friends, can be learned through role-play and practised with their peers, as well as adults. Encourage older children to converse with you regularly to foster conversational skills, including respectfully listening to other viewpoints, and how to pause, think and ask questions.

Let them
be bored!

Children who are curious about learning new things will seldom experience boredom as adults. An enquiring mind keeps us mentally active, which in turn promotes feelings of well-being and self-esteem. Next time your child says, "I'm bored," resist the temptation to provide entertainment for them. Instead, encourage them to use their own imagination to make a list of things they *could* do with the resources that are available to them. Then let them get on with it! You can encourage them further by being an enthusiastic learner yourself and doing activities such as visiting the library together or practising a new skill.

Understanding perspective

Understanding other points of view is essential for building meaningful relationships, and while it doesn't come naturally to many children, it can be developed with a little practice. Next time you're reading with your child, try discussing the characters in the book, as well as what they might be thinking and feeling. For instance, "I wonder what made Oliver act like that," or "Why do Ben and Ameera want to help Mrs Harris?" You can also make observations on real-life situations, such as: "Your brother was really sad he didn't pass his spelling test today. How can we cheer him up?"

Independence

We're often tempted to do things for our children, due to demands on our time, but by acting like this, we're inadvertently sending them the message that we don't have confidence in them, which can affect their self-esteem. Promote independence by:

- Making a list of all the age-appropriate tasks your child could be doing. Ask them which ones they'd like to take responsibility for.

- Tackling the tasks one at a time, so they won't find them overwhelming.

- Ensuring they don't feel rushed, by factoring in extra time to your schedule.

- Encouraging problem-solving skills, if they get stuck.

Don't expect perfection – lower your expectations and praise their effort.

MAKING THEIR OWN DECISIONS (AND MAKING THE RIGHT ONES, TOO!)

Being able to judge a situation and know the right course of action is a skill that develops as children grow up. It helps to promote a sense of independence, as well as encouraging problem-solving and critical-thinking skills. This is especially important as they get older and the decisions they need to make become more significant. You can help your child by:

- **Letting them learn from their mistakes.**
- **Encouraging self-belief and a sense of conviction.**
- **Surrounding them with a supportive network of friends they trust.**
- **Modelling good decision-making skills yourself and discussing these situations with them.**

The more opportunities we give our children to make their own decisions, the better they will become at it as they grow up.

Self-control

Many children struggle with self-control — after all, who wouldn't want to eat their entire birthday cake in one go! But as children grow up, self-discipline is integral to becoming responsible adults and avoiding unhealthy habits. You can help your child by:

- Providing structure and a healthy routine.

- Explaining the reason behind the rules — for example, "If you go to bed too late, you'll be too tired to enjoy the trip to the beach tomorrow."

- If appropriate, letting them experience the consequences of their actions.

- Modelling self-discipline yourself — if you must eat a slab of chocolate, do it in private!

It's also important to praise your child when they use self-control in difficult or frustrating situations. Try saying, "I like how you chose to stay calm," or "Well done for making a sensible decision."

Time management and organization

It's safe to say this doesn't come naturally to many children (!) but the good news is, with a little direction, organization skills can be learned. Make a daily routine checklist so they have something visual they are accountable to – ticking off each task is satisfying and helps to promote a sense of achievement. Ask them to do their tasks in an allotted time – for younger children this is a great way to learn how to tell the time, while older children will practise important time-management skills. Imagine yourself as a mentor rather than a manager – instead of making demands, provide the guidance and support they need to take charge of their own lives.

Standing up for themselves

As adults, we are used to navigating tricky and sometimes socially awkward situations, such as asking for a raise or questioning whether a bill is correct. With young children, it is absolutely right that we should be their biggest advocate, but as they grow older it's important that they learn the skill of being able to speak up for themselves. If your child is shy or reluctant to champion themselves, encourage them to practise with people they know — if they have a problem they need help to solve, get them to ask their teacher for advice, too. Give them lots of opportunities to practise this skill; their confidence will grow and they'll be happier in themselves.

ORIGINAL THINKING AND CREATIVITY

Encouraging a vivid imagination and wondering "what could be" is fundamental – not just because it is an aptitude required in the workplace, but because it helps us to realize our dreams and ambitions. Nurture this skill by encouraging your child to think like an engineer – identify a problem, brainstorm solutions, make a plan and try it out. Give your child a problem to fix creatively, such as:

- **Make a tower with marshmallows, spaghetti and some sticky tape.**
- **Move a toy from one room to another without touching the floor, using cardboard, paper straws, paper clips and string.**
- **Invent something new!**

Encourage your child to see that life is full of multiple solutions and opportunities, all of them unique, and watch their belief in themselves grow.

A sense of humanity

As children grow up, it's important they begin to understand they are part of a bigger picture rather than just focusing on themselves. Having a sense of involvement and acknowledging the part they play in the wider world is essential for well-being. As parents, we can encourage this by giving them responsibility for a family pet or even a houseplant – anything that relies on human input to thrive. We can ask them to help us, if we're struggling with a task, or simply practise empathy ourselves so that we lead by example. These small but powerful acts will help our children to appreciate human connection.

Humility

Having a sense of humility, even when we achieve greatness, is a much respected and valued trait. In a digital world, where bragging is often the norm, cultivating humility helps children to self-regulate their ego. They are also more likely to have better social interactions, and be appreciated and valued by others. We can nurture this trait by encouraging children to use their talents for the benefit of others, such as helping a friend with homework. You can also discourage a sense of entitlement by praising their efforts, rather than giving them a false sense of how exceptional they are.

Intuition

Intuition is difficult to define — a sense of "inner sight" and "trusting your instincts" are often used to describe it. Such an abstract concept can be difficult to explain to children, but as adults we know that listening to a hunch can sometimes be just as advantageous as using logical thinking. The best outcomes often involve an element of both. Try introducing your child to the idea of an "inner voice" that helps them to listen with their whole body and is there to provide useful advice. If they share any insights or feelings with you, always respect and validate them.

CHAPTER 7

Looking to Yourself

From the moment we become parents, we make a
commitment to put the needs of our family first —
but this often leads to us neglecting our own well-
being. Make sure you can draw from your own well
of inner happiness; after all, you cannot
pour from an empty cup.

SELF-CARE

It's easy to push your needs to the bottom of your to-do list, but carving out time to pursue activities that make you happy will have a positive impact on your well-being, meaning you'll be better placed to create a happy family environment for your child. Self-care isn't always about long bubble baths (although those also count!) – instead, view it as any activity that helps you to feel recharged, be that reading a book, pursuing an interest such as crafting or going for a run. The only stipulation is that you spend time doing something for YOU, and only you.

Staying connected

Parenting can be an isolating experience at times, and building a network of family, friends and loved ones helps to provide an additional layer of support when times are tough. Nurturing relationships with other local parents, members of your extended family, or community or church groups helps us to feel connected, which is good for our well-being. As the African proverb: "It takes a village to raise a child" neatly sums up, parenting is a shared responsibility, and if we can give and receive mutual help and support it really does benefit us all.

Celebrating small wins

Parenting can sometimes feel like an uphill struggle. At the end of a hectic day we might even question whether we managed to achieve anything worthwhile! Our perception of "success" changes when we become parents and if we measure ourselves against our pre-children definition of the word, it's easy to become disheartened. Sometimes we forget the small wins we make in our parenting journey every day, such as teaching our child to tie their shoelaces or getting them to bed without any dramas. Getting an older child to put down a gadget and pick up their homework is definitely something worth celebrating! Stay realistic and give yourself some credit – you'll be all the happier for it.

JOMO

We've all heard of FOMO (fear of missing out) but what about JOMO (joy of missing out)? It seems counter-intuitive to enjoy missing out on something, but when we give ourselves some breathing space we can work on looking after ourselves. Sometimes it's good to say no to an invitation, particularly if our days and weeks are already full to bursting with activities and things to do. Finding the time to withdraw and disengage a little from the busyness of our lives gives us the chance to engage with the things that really matter, such as quality one-on-one time with our children.

BECOME YOUR OWN CHEERLEADER

Encouraging your children to be less critical of themselves is second nature, but how critical are you of yourself? If your inner voice is shouting loud, negative thoughts at you, it's time to silence it. When you become aware of your inner critic, start to drown it out with some positivity. Next time you're being hard on yourself, use your positive internal voice to say, "Stop it! That's unhelpful and untrue." Listen to that and focus on positive thoughts. Over time, you'll start to hear the positive voice more frequently, meaning you'll be kinder to yourself.

Be mindful of projecting

Sometimes it's hard not see our children as mini versions of ourselves. By projecting in this way, we inadvertently put pressure on them to be like us or excel at things we weren't able to. By failing to see our children as individuals, we fall into the trap of meeting the needs we think they have (based on our own experiences) rather than providing a parenting approach that is attuned to them as individuals. Let them find their own path and forge their own dreams, knowing that you'll be cheering them on every step of the way.

Create a family routine

Routines are good for all of us. They provide structure that allows us to get tasks done, meaning we can spend more quality time together. Our home environment being organized helps our children to feel safe and looked after. As parents, we'll feel more in control and less stressed, meaning we can focus on the things that are important to us. Sit down together and document a typical day – include regular activities, as well as smaller things you want your children to remember, such as brushing their teeth. Then display the result as a reminder to help keep everyone on track.

Create a strong family unit

A strong family comes from having a shared sense of love, security and connection. The emotional and physical reassurance we gain from this allows us to be ourselves, safe in the knowledge that we are accepted and understood. When children have a secure family unit, it gives them the confidence to discover the world outside. Make your family strong by providing:

- A sense of emotional and physical security.

- Warmth, care and affection.

- A solid routine.

- Firm but fair rules to live by.

- Open channels of communication.

- Connection to each other and others outside the family.

By making sure your family is the strongest it can be, you'll be creating the best environment for happiness to blossom.

APPRECIATING EACH OTHER

Valuing other family members helps to strengthen bonds. Make sure your appreciation levels are set to maximum by trying the following:

- **Ensure that everyone gets a turn to speak during family time and include each person in the conversation. Ask open questions, such as: "What made you feel happy today?"**

- **Regularly talk about family memories — recalling shared experiences is great for bonding and helps children to appreciate life's journey.**

- **Take an interest in each other's achievements and activities.**

- **Acknowledge each other as individuals with a unique skillset.**

This heightened sense of connection to others plays an important role in children's well-being and happiness. A child shown appreciation will learn to appreciate others, as well as learning to value themselves more.

Sharing in the fun times

Spending time together is one of the best things about being part of a family – and bonding and creating special moments is brilliant for boosting our mood. The positive memories that children forge as they grow up will stay with them for a lifetime. Need some inspiration? Try the following:

- Grab a picnic and head for your perfect spot.

- Create a family artwork – buy a canvas and get creative.

- Have a "date" – let your child choose the activity and take them out for dinner afterwards.

Time spent together really is the best investment in your child's future happiness – if done regularly, the happier and more vivid the memories will be.

You are good enough

Parenthood can feel like a never-ending guilt trip. We categorically love our children and want to do the best for them, but at the end of a difficult day when we've been impatient or shouted at them, we feel awful – we've let them down, and we've let ourselves down, too. But know this: perfect parenting is an impossible goal. We're human, so by nature we are flawed. You don't need to be perfect; you simply need to be good enough. Trying your best is all you should be asking of yourself – and it's all your child asks of you, too.

Do more of what makes you happy

It sounds simple: if we want to raise happy and fulfilled children, we have to be happy and fulfilled ourselves. When we put our entire focus on being a parent, though, we can easily lose sight of what makes us, us. By doing this, we're not letting our children know us as individuals with our own unique identities. Don't give up on the things that give your life meaning. Letting our children see us enjoying the company of friends, being close to a partner and pursuing our interests with passion are the best examples of happiness we can give.

DISCIPLINE THE RIGHT WAY

The way we choose to discipline our children when they are young can have long-lasting effects – positive and negative – so it's really important we try to get it right. The old adage "firm but fair" still holds true – simultaneously encouraging independence but placing limits and controls on a child's actions. When your child misbehaves, address the person you know is hidden underneath the little monster screaming in front of you. Explain the reasoning behind the rules and the consequences of their bad behaviour, as well as rewarding demonstrations of responsibility, hard work and good behaviour.

Parenting detox

We've all had those days when we're watching the clock, silently willing it to reach the golden hour of our child's bedtime. Being a parent is rewarding but hard, and it's normal to want to take some time off. If a full-blown minibreak isn't on the horizon right now, make sure you're utilizing those precious evening hours by hitting "reset" and doing something restful. Step away from the temptation to do chores and try:

- Reading a book or your favourite magazine.
- Relaxation exercises, such as yoga or deep breathing.
- Listening to music or a podcast.

Being able to de-stress in this way means that you'll be in a better frame of mind to not only take on the challenges of the following day, but also to embrace the joy of parenting.

Tune in to your child

Parents who are tuned in to their children's needs, and focused on guiding them toward maturity and independence, are more likely to raise happy, resilient children. They are also able to nurture a stronger emotional bond and deeper level of connection. Being "tuned in" means being able to read your child's emotional and behavioural cues, and respond appropriately. What makes them tick? Be sensitive to changes in their tone, expressions and movements. Most importantly, listen to them, and respect their feelings and emotions.

CONCLUSION

Parenting is one of the most rewarding jobs in the world, but it is also one of the toughest. Bringing up confident, resilient and happy children is no mean feat, but the task becomes less daunting and more enriching if we take it one step at a time or, in the case of this book, one tip at a time. Happiness varies from person to person, but at its core is a sense of connection – something that is innate in all parent-and-child relationships. So you're already most of the way there...

Notes

HELP YOUR CHILD MAKE FRIENDS

Poppy O'Neill

ISBN: 978-1-78783-665-5

£9.99 UK, $13.99 US, $15.99 CAN

SEEING YOUR CHILD STRUGGLE TO MAKE FRIENDS IS DIFFICULT FOR ANYONE

Friendships can be tricky, but help is at hand. This guide will help you teach your child what makes a healthy friendship, and equip them with the tools they need to build stronger bonds and feel more confident in making new friends. Offering ideas, information and simple tips that will help you talk to your child and show them how to develop their social skills, this book will ensure they enjoy better friendships for life.

HELP YOUR CHILD DE-STRESS

Vicki Vrint

ISBN: 978-1-78783-673-0

£9.99 UK, $13.99 US, $15.99 CAN

72% OF CHILDREN SHOW BEHAVIOURS LINKED TO STRESS

Small amounts of stress are normal, but it can be difficult to know how best to support a child when they feel overwhelmed with worry. This practical guide offers strategies to help alleviate the physical symptoms and emotional signs of stress. By adopting simple tips, lifestyle changes and mood-boosting activities, you can help your child overcome challenging situations and live a happy and more carefree life.

Have you enjoyed this book?

If so, why not write a review on your favourite website? If you're interested in finding out more about our books, find us on Facebook at **Summersdale Publishers** and follow us on Twitter at **@Summersdale**.

Thanks very much for buying this Summersdale book.

www.summersdale.com

IMAGE CREDITS

watercolour balloon © Elena__Efremova/Shutterstock.com
balloon outline throughout © krissikunterbunt/Shutterstock.com